MARKETING MASTERY

UNLOCKING THE SECRETS OF MODERN MARKETING

DR. JAGADEESH PILLAI

Made with ♥ on the Notion Press Platform
www.notionpress.com

|| Dedicated to all wisdom seekers around the world ||

ေ

Contents

Contents

PRAYER

"Om Bhadram Karnebhih Shrunuyaama DevaahBhadram Pashyemaakshabhiryajatraah SthirairangaistushtuvaamsastanoobhihVyashema Devahitam YadaayuhSwasti Na Indro VridhashravaahSwasti Nah Pooshaa VishwavedaahSwasti Nastaarkshyo ArishtanemihSwasti No Brihaspatir DadhaatuOm Shantih, Shantih, Shantih"

The literal meaning of this mantra is: OM. O Gods! Let us hear auspicious words from our ears. O reverent Gods! Let us behold propitious visions from our eyes, let our organs and body be stable, healthy, and strong. Let us do that which is pleasing to the gods in the life span allotted to us. May Indra, inscribed in the scriptures, bring us fortune! May Pushan, the knower of the world, grant us prosperity! May Trakshya, who vanquishes enemies, bestow us with blessings! May Brihaspati bring us success!
OM Peace, Peace, Peace.

About The Author

Dr. Jagadeesh Pillai is a renowned Guinness World Record holder, writer, and researcher hailing from Varanasi, also known as the abode of Lord Shiva. With a Ph.D. in Vedic Science and a range of creative ideas and achievements, he is a true polymath. He is the author of more than 100 books including Research Publications. Although his roots can be traced back to Kerala, the people of Varanasi hold him in high regard and affectionately consider him one of their own.

In 1998, Dr. Pillai was offered a job at Banaras Hindu University, but he left the position after only two months to pursue greater goals in life. He believed that in order to study Indian scriptures and engage in other creative endeavours, he needed to retire from the daily grind of working solely for money at a young age.

He started an export business from scratch, using the knowledge he had gained from a previous job in the industry. His intelligence and unique approach to business led to great success in a short period of time, earning him more in just a decade and a half than he would have in a lifetime working in a government job. Upon the passing of Dr. APJ Abdul Kalam, Dr. Pillai decided to leave the business and dedicate himself to reading, studying, researching, and experimenting.

During his tenure in the export business, Dr. Pillai traveled to over 16 countries, gaining valuable insight and experiencing the world and life in detail.

Dr. Pillai has achieved four Guinness World Records in the following subjects:

"Script to Screen" - In this record, Dr. Pillai produced and directed an animation film within the shortest time possible, breaking the previous record set by Canadians. He has also received numerous national and international awards and recognitions for this achievement.

Longest Line of Postcards - For this record, Dr. Pillai created a line of 16,300 postcards on the occasion of the 163rd anniversary of Indian Postal Day. The event also included a questionnaire about the Indian flag.

Largest Poster Awareness Campaign - Dr. Pillai designed an awareness campaign on the subject of "Beti Bachao - Beti Padhao" (Save the Girl Child - Educate the Girl Child) to achieve this record.

Largest Envelope - In tribute to the Indian Prime Minister's "Make in India" initiative, Dr. Pillai created a 4000 square meter envelope using waste paper to achieve this record.

Attempted - **70000 Candles on a 210 kg Cake** - To celebrate the 70th Indian Independence Day, Dr. Pillai attempted to light 70,000 candles on a 210 kg cake, which was recorded in World Records India.

Attempted - **Documentary on Dhamek Stupa of Sarnath in 17 Languages** - Dr. Pillai attempted to create a documentary on the Dhamek Stupa of Sarnath, dubbing it in 17 different languages. The result of this attempt is currently awaiting confirmation from the Guinness World Records.

Dr. Pillai is skilled in teaching the Bhagavad Gita, a Hindu scripture, and is popular among young people. He has helped many young people improve their lives through his motivational teachings.

In addition to teaching, he has composed and sung numerous Sanskrit Bhajans and patriotic songs.

He has also written and directed several short films and documentaries for awareness campaigns, and has volunteered with the police in both UP and Kerala to spread awareness about various issues through videos and photography.

Incredibly, he has produced and directed over 100 documentaries about the city of Varanasi, all on his own.

He has also helped and guided more than 25 boys and girls to achieve world records through creative and innovative methods. He is a multifaceted person who uses his intellect and the blessings given to him by God to excel in various areas. He is both a teacher and a student, always learning and teaching, and is able to master any subject he comes across.

He is a selfless social activist and motivational speaker who has overcome struggles and failures to become a successful and enthusiastic individual with a rich life experience.

In addition to his work with the Bhagavad Gita, he is also an efficient Tarot card reader, Astro-Vastu consultant, and a talented singer and composer. He has sung the entire Ram Charita Manas and Bhagavad Gita in his own compositions, and has sung the phrase "Lokah Samastha Sukhino Bhavantu" in 50 different languages. He is currently working on a detailed and scientific study of Vedas, Upanishads, Puranas, and the Bhagavad Gita. He has also composed and sung the Hanuman Chalisa and Gayatri Mantra in 108 and 1008 different compositions, respectively.

Awards - Four Times Guinness World Records, Winner of Mahatma Gandhi Vishwa Shanti Puraskar, Mahatma Gandhi Global Peace Ambassador, Kashi Ratna Award, Dr. APJ Abdul Kalam Motivational Person of the Year 2017, Mother Teresa Award, Indira Gandhi Priyadarshini Award, Bharat Vikas Ratna Award, Udyog Ratna Award, Vigyan Prasar Award, Poorvanchal Ratn Samman.

PREFACE

Are you ready to unlock the secrets of modern marketing? If so, then this book is for you. Marketing Mastery: Unlocking the Secrets of Modern Marketing is an essential guide for anyone looking to gain a comprehensive understanding of the modern marketing landscape.

This book provides an in-depth look at the strategies, tactics, and tools used by today's top marketers. It covers everything from the basics of digital marketing to the latest trends in social media and content marketing. It also provides practical advice on how to create effective campaigns and measure their success.

Whether you're a beginner or an experienced marketer, this book will help you gain the knowledge and skills you need to succeed in today's competitive marketing environment. With its comprehensive coverage and easy-to-follow instructions, you'll be able to quickly master the fundamentals of modern marketing and start achieving your goals.

So, if you're ready to take your marketing skills to the next level, then this book is for you. Unlock the secrets of modern marketing and start achieving success today.

I

Introduction to Marketing

Marketing is the process of creating, communicating, and delivering value to customers. It involves understanding customer needs and developing products and services to meet those needs. It also involves creating a brand identity and building relationships with customers.

At its core, marketing is about understanding the customer and creating a strategy to reach them. It involves researching the target market, understanding their needs, and developing a plan to reach them. It also involves creating a brand identity and building relationships with customers.

Marketing is a dynamic field that is constantly evolving. It requires an understanding of the latest trends and technologies, as well as an ability to think strategically. It also requires creativity and an understanding of the customer.

Marketing is a complex field that requires a deep understanding of the customer and the market. It involves understanding customer needs, developing products and services to meet those needs, and creating a brand identity. It also involves understanding the latest trends and technologies, as well as an ability to think strategically.

Marketing Mastery: Unlocking the Secrets of Modern Marketing will provide readers with an in-depth look at the strategies and techniques used by today's top marketers. It will provide readers with the knowledge and skills they need to become successful marketers. It will also provide readers with the tools and resources they need to stay ahead of the competition.

II

Consumer Behavior

Consumer behavior is a key component of modern marketing. It is the study of how individuals, groups, and organizations make decisions about what products and services to purchase, use, and dispose of. Understanding consumer behavior is essential for marketers to effectively reach their target audience and create successful marketing campaigns.

Consumer behavior is influenced by a variety of factors, including cultural, social, psychological, and personal. Cultural influences include values, beliefs, and norms that are shared among a group of people. Social influences include family, friends, and peers. Psychological influences include motivation, perception, and learning. Personal influences include lifestyle, personality, and attitudes.

Marketers must understand how these factors influence

consumer behavior in order to create effective marketing campaigns. For example, marketers must consider cultural influences when creating campaigns for different cultures. They must also consider social influences when targeting specific groups of people. Additionally, marketers must consider psychological and personal influences when creating campaigns that appeal to the motivations, perceptions, and attitudes of their target audience.

By understanding consumer behavior, marketers can create campaigns that are tailored to their target audience and are more likely to be successful. They can also use consumer behavior to identify new opportunities and develop strategies to capitalize on them. By leveraging consumer behavior, marketers can create campaigns that are more effective and efficient, resulting in increased sales and profits.

In conclusion, consumer behavior is an essential component of modern marketing. By understanding how cultural, social, psychological, and personal influences affect consumer behavior, marketers can create campaigns that are tailored to their target audience and are more likely to be successful. By leveraging consumer behavior, marketers can create campaigns that are more effective and efficient, resulting in increased sales and profits.

III

Market Research

Market research is an essential component of modern marketing. It helps marketers understand their target audience, identify potential opportunities, and develop effective strategies. By gathering data and analyzing it, marketers can gain valuable insights into their customers' needs and preferences.

Market research can be conducted in a variety of ways, including surveys, focus groups, interviews, and online research. Surveys are a great way to collect data from a large number of people quickly and efficiently. Focus groups allow marketers to gain a deeper understanding of their target audience by engaging in conversations with a small group of people. Interviews are a great way to gain a more personal understanding of a customer's needs and preferences. Online research can be used to gain insights into customer behavior and trends.

No matter which method of market research is used, it is important to ensure that the data collected is accurate and reliable. Marketers should also be aware of any ethical considerations when conducting market research.

By leveraging the power of market research, marketers can gain valuable insights into their target audience and develop effective strategies to reach them. Market research can help marketers understand their customers' needs and preferences, identify potential opportunities, and develop effective strategies to reach their target audience. By understanding their customers, marketers can create campaigns that are tailored to their target audience and maximize their return on investment.

IV

Segmentation, Targeting, and Positioning

Segmentation, targeting, and positioning are three essential components of modern marketing. Segmentation is the process of dividing a market into distinct groups of customers with similar needs and characteristics. Targeting is the process of selecting one or more segments to pursue. Positioning is the process of creating a unique image of a product or service in the minds of customers.

When it comes to segmentation, marketers must identify the characteristics of their target market and determine how to best divide it into distinct segments. This can be done by analyzing customer demographics, psychographics, and behaviors. Once the market is segmented, marketers can then select one or more segments to target. This requires an understanding of the needs and preferences of each segment and how they differ from one another.

Positioning is the process of creating a unique image of a product or service in the minds of customers. This involves developing a unique value proposition and creating a distinct brand identity. It also involves communicating the value proposition to the target market in a way that resonates with them.

By understanding and applying the principles of segmentation, targeting, and positioning, marketers can create effective marketing strategies that will help them reach their desired goals. By segmenting their target market, they can identify the most profitable segments and target them with the right message. By positioning their product or service in the minds of customers, they can create a unique image that will help them stand out from the competition.

Segmentation, targeting, and positioning are essential components of modern marketing. By understanding and applying these principles, marketers can create effective strategies that will help them reach their desired goals. With the right approach, they can unlock the secrets of modern marketing and create a successful marketing campaign.

V

Branding

Branding is an essential component of modern marketing. It is the process of creating a unique identity for a product, service, or company that sets it apart from its competitors. A successful brand will create an emotional connection with its target audience, allowing them to recognize and remember the product or service.

At its core, branding is about creating a memorable and recognizable image for a product or service. This can be done through the use of logos, slogans, and other visual elements. It is also important to create a consistent message across all marketing channels, including social media, print, and digital.

Branding is also about creating an emotional connection with customers. This can be done through storytelling, creating a unique voice, and using visuals that evoke emotion. It is also important to create a consistent message across all marketing channels, including social media, print, and digital.

The goal of branding is to create a strong and lasting impression on customers. This can be done by creating a unique identity, creating a consistent message, and using visuals that evoke emotion. It is also important to create a consistent message across all marketing channels, including social media, print, and digital.

Branding is an essential part of modern marketing and can be used to create a strong and lasting impression on customers. By creating a unique identity, creating a consistent message, and using visuals that evoke emotion, brands can create an emotional connection with their target audience. This connection will help customers recognize and remember the product or service, leading to increased sales and customer loyalty.

VI

Product Development and Management

Product development and management is a critical component of modern marketing. It involves the creation of new products or services, as well as the management of existing ones. It is essential for businesses to stay competitive in today's ever-changing market.

Product development involves researching customer needs and wants, designing a product or service to meet those needs, and then testing and refining the product or service. It is important to ensure that the product or service is of high quality and meets customer expectations.

Product management involves the ongoing management of the product or service. This includes monitoring customer feedback, making changes to the product or service as needed, and ensuring that the product or service is meeting customer needs. It also involves marketing the product or service to potential customers.

Product development and management is a complex process that requires a deep understanding of customer needs and wants, as well as the ability to create and manage products or services that meet those needs. It is essential for businesses to stay competitive in today's ever-changing market.

Product development and management is a key component of modern marketing. It involves researching customer needs and wants, designing a product or service to meet those needs, and then testing and refining the product or service. It also involves ongoing management of the product or service, including monitoring customer feedback, making changes to the product or service as needed, and marketing the product or service to potential customers.

Product development and management is a complex process that requires a deep understanding of customer needs and wants, as well as the ability to create and manage products or services that meet those needs. It is essential for businesses to stay competitive in today's ever-evolving market. By mastering the art of product development and management, businesses can gain a competitive edge and unlock the secrets of modern marketing.

VII

Pricing Strategy

Pricing strategy is a critical component of any successful marketing plan. It is essential to understand the various pricing models available and how to use them to maximize profits. By understanding the different pricing strategies, businesses can create a competitive advantage and increase their market share.

The most common pricing strategies are cost-plus pricing, market-based pricing, and value-based pricing. Cost-plus pricing is when a business sets a price based on the cost of production plus a markup. Market-based pricing is when a business sets a price based on what the market will bear. Value-based pricing is when a business sets a price based on the perceived value of the product or service.

When deciding on a pricing strategy, businesses should consider their target market, the competition, and the cost of production. It is important to understand the customer's needs and wants and how they compare to the competition. Additionally, businesses should consider the cost of production and the potential profit margin.

Businesses should also consider the impact of pricing on their brand. A low price may attract more customers, but it could also damage the brand's reputation. On the other hand, a high price may limit the number of customers, but it could also increase the perceived value of the product or service.

Finally, businesses should consider the impact of pricing on their long-term goals. A pricing strategy should be designed to maximize profits over the long-term, not just in the short-term.

Pricing strategy is a complex and ever-evolving process. By understanding the different pricing models and how to use them to maximize profits, businesses can create a competitive advantage and increase their market share. With the right pricing strategy, businesses can unlock the secrets of modern marketing and achieve success.

VIII

Distribution and Channel Management

Distribution and channel management are essential components of modern marketing. By understanding the different types of distribution channels and how to effectively manage them, businesses can maximize their reach and increase their sales.

Distribution channels are the pathways through which products and services are delivered to customers. They can be divided into two main categories: direct and indirect. Direct channels involve the direct sale of products and services to customers, while indirect channels involve the use of intermediaries such as wholesalers, retailers, and distributors.

Channel management is the process of managing the

different distribution channels to ensure that products and services are delivered to customers in an efficient and cost-effective manner. This includes selecting the right channels, setting up the necessary infrastructure, and managing the relationships between the different parties involved.

When it comes to channel management, businesses must consider a number of factors. These include the cost of distribution, the availability of resources, the customer's preferences, and the competitive landscape. Additionally, businesses must also consider the impact of technology on distribution and channel management.

In order to maximize the effectiveness of their distribution and channel management strategies, businesses must have a clear understanding of their target market and the channels that are best suited to reach them. They must also be aware of the latest trends in the industry and be prepared to adapt their strategies accordingly.

By understanding the importance of distribution and channel management, businesses can unlock the secrets of modern marketing and maximize their reach and sales. With the right strategies in place, businesses can ensure that their products and services are delivered to customers in an efficient and cost-effective manner.

IX

Promotion and Advertising

Promotion and advertising are essential components of modern marketing. Without them, businesses would struggle to reach their target audiences and generate sales. To truly master marketing, it is important to understand the different types of promotion and advertising available, and how to use them effectively.

Traditional forms of promotion and advertising, such as print, radio, and television, are still widely used today. Print advertising includes newspapers, magazines, and billboards, while radio and television advertising can be used to reach a wide audience. These forms of promotion and advertising can be expensive, but they can also be highly effective when used correctly.

Digital promotion and advertising have become increasingly popular in recent years. Social media platforms, such as Facebook, Twitter, and Instagram, are great ways to reach potential customers and build relationships with them. Search engine optimization (SEO) is also an important part of digital promotion and advertising, as it helps businesses to appear higher in search engine results.

In addition to traditional and digital promotion and advertising, businesses can also use guerrilla marketing tactics to reach their target audiences. Guerrilla marketing involves using unconventional methods to promote a product or service, such as using street art, flash mobs, or viral videos.

No matter which type of promotion and advertising a business chooses, it is important to ensure that the message is clear and consistent. It is also important to track the results of each campaign to determine which methods are most effective. By understanding the different types of promotion and advertising available, businesses can unlock the secrets of modern marketing and maximize their success.

X

Public Relations and Corporate Communications

Public relations and corporate communications are essential components of modern marketing. They are the tools used to create and maintain relationships between a company and its stakeholders, including customers, employees, investors, and the public.

Public relations involves creating and managing a company's public image. This includes crafting press releases, managing media relations, and developing campaigns to promote the company's products and services. Corporate communications, on the other hand, focuses on internal communication, such as employee newsletters, intranet content, and internal memos.

Both public relations and corporate communications are

essential for a successful marketing strategy. Public relations helps to build trust and credibility with the public, while corporate communications helps to ensure that employees are informed and engaged. By leveraging both of these tools, companies can create a positive public image and foster strong relationships with their stakeholders.

In addition, public relations and corporate communications can be used to create a unified message across all channels. By creating a consistent message, companies can ensure that their message is heard and understood by their target audience. This can help to build brand loyalty and trust, which are essential for any successful marketing campaign.

Public relations and corporate communications are powerful tools that can help companies to reach their marketing goals. By leveraging these tools, companies can create a positive public image, foster strong relationships with their stakeholders, and create a unified message across all channels. With the right strategy, companies can unlock the secrets of modern marketing and achieve success.

XI
Digital Marketing

Digital marketing is a powerful tool for businesses of all sizes, allowing them to reach a wide audience and build relationships with customers. In today's digital age, it is essential for businesses to have a strong digital presence in order to remain competitive.

Digital marketing encompasses a variety of strategies, including search engine optimization (SEO), content marketing, social media marketing, email marketing, and more. SEO is the process of optimizing a website to rank higher in search engine results, while content marketing involves creating and sharing content to engage customers and build relationships. Social media marketing involves creating and sharing content on social media platforms to reach a wider audience, while email marketing involves sending emails to customers to keep them informed and engaged.

No matter the size of the business, digital marketing can be used to reach a wide audience and build relationships with customers. It is important to understand the different strategies and how they can be used to reach the desired goals. For example, SEO can be used to increase website traffic, while content marketing can be used to build relationships with customers.

Digital marketing also allows businesses to track and measure their success. By using analytics tools, businesses can track the performance of their campaigns and make adjustments as needed. This allows businesses to optimize their campaigns and ensure they are reaching their desired goals.

Digital marketing is an essential part of modern marketing and can be used to reach a wide audience and build relationships with customers. By understanding the different strategies and how they can be used, businesses can create effective campaigns that will help them reach their desired goals. With the right strategies and tools, businesses can unlock the secrets of modern marketing and take their business to the next level.

XII

Social Media Marketing

Social media marketing is a powerful tool that can be used to create a strong online presence. It can be used to create engaging content, build relationships with customers, and increase brand visibility. Companies can use social media to share news, updates, and promotions, as well as to interact with customers and build relationships.

When it comes to social media marketing, it is important to create a strategy that is tailored to the company's goals. Companies should consider their target audience, the type of content they want to share, and the platforms they want to use. It is also important to create a content calendar that outlines when and how often content should be posted.

When creating content, it is important to focus on quality over quantity. Companies should create content that is engaging, informative, and relevant to their target audience. Companies should also use visuals, such as images and videos, to make their content more engaging.

Finally, companies should measure the success of their social media marketing efforts. Companies should track metrics such as engagement, reach, and conversions to determine which strategies are working and which need to be improved.

Social media marketing is an essential tool for businesses of all sizes. By creating a tailored strategy, creating engaging content, and measuring success, companies can unlock the secrets of modern marketing and increase their online presence.

XIII

Search Engine Optimization (SEO)

Search Engine Optimization (SEO) is an essential component of modern marketing. It is the process of optimizing a website to increase its visibility in search engine results, thus driving more organic traffic to the website. SEO involves a variety of techniques, including keyword research, content optimization, link building, and more.

When it comes to SEO, the goal is to make sure that your website is visible to the right people. This means optimizing your website for the right keywords, creating content that is relevant to your target audience, and building links from other websites that are related to your niche.

SEO is a complex process, but it is essential for any business that wants to succeed in the modern marketing landscape. By optimizing your website for search engines, you can increase your visibility and reach more potential customers.

When it comes to SEO, it is important to remember that it is an ongoing process. You need to constantly monitor your website's performance and make adjustments as needed. Additionally, you should keep up with the latest trends in SEO and make sure that your website is up-to-date with the latest algorithms and best practices.

SEO is a powerful tool for any business that wants to succeed in the modern marketing landscape. By optimizing your website for search engines, you can increase your visibility and reach more potential customers. With the right strategies and techniques, you can unlock the secrets of modern marketing and take your business to the next level.

XIV
Email Marketing

Email marketing is a powerful tool for modern marketers. It allows them to reach a wide audience quickly and cost-effectively. With the right strategy, email marketing can be an effective way to build relationships with customers, increase brand awareness, and drive sales.

At its core, email marketing is about sending emails to a list of subscribers. These emails can be used to promote products, share news, or provide valuable content. To be successful, marketers must create compelling emails that are tailored to their audience. This means understanding their needs and interests, and crafting messages that are relevant and engaging.

When it comes to email marketing, there are several key elements to consider. First, marketers must create an effective email list. This means collecting contact information from potential customers and segmenting the list into different groups. This allows marketers to send targeted emails to the right people.

Second, marketers must craft compelling emails. This means writing engaging subject lines, using attractive visuals, and providing valuable content. It's also important to optimize emails for mobile devices, as many people now access their emails on their phones.

Finally, marketers must measure the success of their email campaigns. This means tracking open rates, click-through rates, and other metrics. This data can be used to refine future campaigns and ensure that they are as effective as possible.

Email marketing is an essential part of modern marketing. With the right strategy, it can be an effective way to reach customers, build relationships, and drive sales. By understanding the key elements of email marketing and optimizing campaigns for success, marketers can unlock the power of this powerful tool.

XV

Content Marketing

Content marketing is a powerful tool for modern marketers, allowing them to reach their target audience in a meaningful and cost-effective way. By creating and distributing valuable, relevant, and consistent content, marketers can attract and retain a clearly defined audience, while driving profitable customer action.

At its core, content marketing is about creating and sharing content that is valuable to your target audience. This content can come in many forms, including blog posts, videos, podcasts, infographics, and more. Content marketing is not about selling, but rather about providing useful information that helps to build trust and loyalty with your audience.

When done correctly, content marketing can be an incredibly effective way to reach your target audience. It can help to build relationships with potential customers, increase brand awareness, and drive conversions. Additionally, content marketing can help to improve search engine rankings, as search engines reward websites that provide valuable content.

Content marketing is not a one-size-fits-all solution, however. It requires careful planning and execution to ensure that the content you create is relevant to your target audience and provides value. Additionally, content marketing requires ongoing effort to ensure that your content remains fresh and up-to-date.

In order to maximize the effectiveness of your content marketing efforts, it is important to have a clear understanding of your target audience and their needs. Additionally, you should create a content marketing strategy that outlines your goals, objectives, and tactics. Finally, you should measure the success of your content marketing efforts to ensure that you are achieving your desired results.

Content marketing is an essential part of any modern marketing strategy. By creating and distributing valuable, relevant, and consistent content, marketers can build relationships with their target audience, increase brand awareness, and drive conversions. With careful planning and execution, content marketing can be an incredibly effective way to reach your target audience and achieve your desired results.

Content marketing is all about creating and sharing content that is valuable and relevant to your target audience, and that aligns with your overall business goals. This can include blog posts, articles, infographics, videos, podcasts, and more. The goal is to provide value to your audience and build trust and credibility with them, rather than solely pushing sales or promotional messages.

One of the key benefits of content marketing is that it can help to establish your brand as a thought leader in your industry. By consistently producing high-quality content that addresses the needs and concerns of your target audience, you can position yourself as a trusted source of information and a go-to resource for your industry.

Another benefit of content marketing is that it can help to drive traffic and conversions to your website. By including calls-to-action and other conversion-optimized elements in your content, you can encourage your audience to take a desired action, such as making a purchase or signing up for your email list.

Content marketing also helps in SEO, by creating high-quality, keyword-rich content, you can help to improve your search engine rankings and drive more organic traffic to your website. Additionally, by sharing your content on social media and other channels, you can expand your reach and attract new visitors to your site.

However, content marketing is not a one-time effort, it requires consistent and regular effort. It's important to have a content marketing plan in place that outlines your goals, target audience, and content strategy, and to regularly measure and analyze your results to ensure that your efforts are paying off.

Overall, content marketing is an essential part of any modern marketing strategy, that helps to build relationships with your target audience, establish your brand as a thought leader, and drive conversions and traffic to your website.

XVI
Influencer Marketing

Influencer marketing has become an increasingly popular tool for businesses to reach their target audiences. By leveraging the power of influencers, companies can tap into a vast network of potential customers and create a powerful marketing campaign.

At its core, influencer marketing is a form of marketing that focuses on leveraging the influence of key individuals to promote a product or service. Influencers are typically people who have a large following on social media, such as celebrities, bloggers, and YouTube stars. By partnering with influencers, businesses can reach a much larger audience than they would be able to reach on their own.

The key to successful influencer marketing is to find the right influencers for your brand. It is important to find influencers who are passionate about your product or service and who have a large and engaged following. Once you have identified the right influencers, you can create a campaign that is tailored to their audience.

When creating an influencer marketing campaign, it is important to focus on creating content that is engaging and relevant to the influencer's audience. This could include creating videos, blog posts, or social media posts that feature the influencer. Additionally, it is important to ensure that the influencer is compensated for their work.

Finally, it is important to measure the success of your influencer marketing campaign. This can be done by tracking the number of followers, likes, and shares that the influencer's content receives. Additionally, you can measure the success of your campaign by tracking the number of sales or leads that it generates.

Influencer marketing is a powerful tool for businesses to reach their target audiences. By leveraging the influence of key individuals, businesses can create a powerful marketing campaign that can reach a much larger audience than they would be able to reach on their own. Influencer marketing can be especially effective in building brand awareness, increasing engagement, and driving sales.

One of the key benefits of influencer marketing is that it allows businesses to tap into the trust and credibility of influencers, who are often seen as experts in their field or niche. By working with influencers, businesses can gain access to their followers and audiences, who are likely to be more engaged and responsive to the influencer's recommendations.

Another benefit of influencer marketing is that it can be highly targeted. By working with influencers who have an audience that aligns with a business's target market, businesses can ensure that their marketing efforts are reaching the right people. Additionally, influencer marketing can be more cost-effective than traditional forms of advertising, as it often requires a smaller investment.

However, it's important for businesses to be selective about the influencers they work with, and to ensure that the influencer aligns with their brand and message. It's also important for businesses to monitor their campaigns and measure the results, to ensure that they are getting a good return on their investment.

Overall, influencer marketing can be a powerful tool for businesses to reach and engage with their target audiences, and it is a cost-effective way to expand the reach of the business and build brand awareness and drive sales.

XVII
Affiliate Marketing

Affiliate marketing is a powerful tool for modern marketers. It is a type of performance-based marketing in which a business rewards one or more affiliates for each customer or visitor brought by the affiliate's own marketing efforts. Affiliate marketing is a great way to reach a wide audience and generate more sales.

At its core, affiliate marketing is a simple concept. A business pays an affiliate for each customer or visitor they bring to their website. The affiliate then promotes the business's products or services to their own audience, and when a sale is made, the affiliate receives a commission. This commission-based system allows businesses to reach a larger audience and increase their sales without having to invest in expensive advertising campaigns.

Affiliate marketing is a great way to build relationships with customers. By partnering with affiliates, businesses can create a network of loyal customers who are more likely to purchase their products or services. Affiliates can also help businesses reach new customers by promoting their products or services to their own audiences.

Affiliate marketing is also a great way to increase brand awareness. By partnering with affiliates, businesses can reach a larger audience and create more visibility for their brand. This increased visibility can lead to more sales and more customers.

Affiliate marketing is a great way to increase sales and build relationships with customers. By partnering with affiliates, businesses can reach a larger audience, create more visibility for their brand, and generate more sales. With the right strategies and tactics, businesses can use affiliate marketing to unlock the secrets of modern marketing and take their business to the next level.

XVIII
Mobile Marketing

Mobile marketing is a powerful tool for businesses of all sizes. It allows companies to reach their target audiences in a cost-effective and efficient manner. By leveraging the latest technologies, businesses can create engaging campaigns that drive conversions and increase brand awareness.

The key to successful mobile marketing is understanding the needs of your target audience. Knowing who your customers are and what they want is essential for creating effective campaigns. Once you have identified your target audience, you can create campaigns that are tailored to their needs.

When it comes to mobile marketing, there are a variety of strategies that can be used. From SMS campaigns to mobile apps, businesses can use a variety of tactics to reach their target audiences. Additionally, businesses can use location-based marketing to target customers in specific areas.

In addition to creating campaigns, businesses must also measure the success of their mobile marketing efforts. By tracking key metrics such as click-through rates and conversions, businesses can determine which strategies are working and which need to be improved.

Finally, businesses must ensure that their mobile marketing campaigns are compliant with all applicable laws and regulations. This includes ensuring that all data is collected and stored securely, and that customers are given the opportunity to opt-out of any campaigns.

Mobile marketing is an essential tool for businesses of all sizes. By understanding the needs of their target audiences and leveraging the latest technologies, businesses can create effective campaigns that drive conversions and increase brand awareness. By measuring the success of their campaigns and ensuring compliance with all applicable laws and regulations, businesses can ensure that their mobile marketing efforts are successful.

XIX

Marketing Analytics

Marketing analytics is a powerful tool for modern marketers. It allows them to gain insights into customer behavior, identify trends, and measure the success of their campaigns. By leveraging data-driven insights, marketers can make informed decisions that will help them reach their goals.

Analytics can be used to track customer engagement, measure the effectiveness of campaigns, and identify areas of improvement. It can also be used to identify customer segments, target specific audiences, and optimize marketing strategies.

Analytics can be used to measure the success of campaigns, identify areas of improvement, and optimize marketing strategies. It can also be used to track customer engagement, measure the effectiveness of campaigns, and identify customer segments. By leveraging data-driven insights, marketers can make informed decisions that will help them reach their goals.

Analytics can also be used to identify trends in customer behavior, such as which products are most popular, which channels are most effective, and which campaigns are most successful. This information can be used to create more effective campaigns and target specific audiences.

Analytics can also be used to measure the ROI of campaigns, identify areas of improvement, and optimize marketing strategies. By leveraging data-driven insights, marketers can make informed decisions that will help them reach their goals.

In conclusion, marketing analytics is a powerful tool for modern marketers. It allows them to gain insights into customer behavior, identify trends, measure the success of their campaigns, and optimize their strategies. By leveraging data-driven insights, marketers can make informed decisions that will help them reach their goals and unlock the secrets of modern marketing.

XX

Marketing Automation

Marketing automation is a powerful tool for modern marketers. It allows them to streamline their marketing processes, save time, and increase efficiency. With marketing automation, marketers can automate tasks such as email campaigns, social media posts, and website updates. This helps them to focus on more strategic tasks and free up time for other activities.

Marketing automation also helps marketers to better target their audiences. By using automated segmentation, marketers can create personalized messages for each segment of their audience. This helps to ensure that their messages are more relevant and effective. Additionally, marketing automation can help marketers to track and measure the success of their campaigns. This allows them to make adjustments and optimize their campaigns for better results.

Finally, marketing automation can help marketers to save money. By automating tasks, marketers can reduce their labor costs and free up resources for other activities. Additionally, marketing automation can help marketers to reduce their marketing costs by eliminating the need for manual processes.

In short, marketing automation is an invaluable tool for modern marketers. It helps them to streamline their processes, save time, and increase efficiency. It also helps them to better target their audiences and track and measure the success of their campaigns. Finally, it can help them to save money by reducing their labor costs and marketing costs. With marketing automation, modern marketers can unlock the secrets of modern marketing and take their campaigns to the next level.

XXI

International Marketing

International marketing is a powerful tool for businesses looking to expand their reach and increase their profits. It involves the strategic use of marketing techniques to reach customers in different countries and cultures. By understanding the nuances of international markets, businesses can create effective campaigns that will resonate with their target audiences.

At its core, international marketing is about understanding the needs and wants of customers in different countries and cultures. It requires an in-depth knowledge of the local market, including the language, customs, and values of the target audience. Companies must also be aware of the legal and regulatory requirements of each country, as well as the competitive landscape.

Successful international marketing campaigns require

careful planning and execution. Companies must develop a comprehensive strategy that takes into account the unique needs of each market. This includes researching the target audience, developing a marketing mix that resonates with them, and creating a budget that allows for the necessary resources.

In addition to traditional marketing techniques, companies must also consider digital marketing strategies. This includes leveraging social media, search engine optimization, and other digital channels to reach customers in different countries. Companies must also be aware of the cultural differences between countries and tailor their campaigns accordingly.

International marketing is a complex and ever-evolving field. Companies must stay up-to-date on the latest trends and technologies to ensure their campaigns are successful. By understanding the nuances of international markets and leveraging the right marketing techniques, businesses can unlock the secrets of modern marketing and expand their reach around the world.

XXII
Trade Marketing

Trade marketing is a powerful tool for businesses to reach their target audience and increase their sales. It involves the strategic use of promotional activities, such as discounts, special offers, and product placement, to drive sales and increase brand awareness. Trade marketing is a key component of any successful marketing strategy, as it helps to build relationships with customers and create a positive brand image.

Trade marketing is a complex process that requires careful planning and execution. It involves understanding the needs of the target audience, developing a strategy to reach them, and then executing the plan. It also requires a deep understanding of the competitive landscape and the ability to identify opportunities to differentiate the brand from its competitors.

The success of a trade marketing campaign depends on the ability to create a compelling message that resonates with the target audience. This requires an understanding of the customer's needs and preferences, as well as the ability to craft a message that speaks to them. Additionally, trade marketing campaigns must be tailored to the specific needs of the target audience, as well as the competitive landscape.

Trade marketing also requires a deep understanding of the customer journey. This includes understanding the customer's buying process, as well as the channels they use to make their purchase. Additionally, trade marketing campaigns must be tailored to the customer's needs and preferences, as well as the competitive landscape.

Finally, trade marketing campaigns must be tracked and measured to ensure that they are achieving the desired results. This includes tracking the effectiveness of the campaign, as well as the customer's response to it. By tracking and measuring the success of a trade marketing campaign, businesses can make adjustments to ensure that they are reaching their target audience and achieving their desired results

Trade marketing is also an essential aspect of any business. It is the process of stimulating increased demand from wholesalers, retailers, and other members of the supply chain and aims to ensure that products and services remain competitive and profitable. Trade marketing is the bridge between manufacturers and channel partners, retailers, and global markets.

The objectives of trade marketing include increasing distribution, improving product visibility, and enhancing relationships with channel partners. By understanding various distribution channels, manufacturers can provide appropriate resources such as sales and marketing training, assortment planning, and advertising support to retailers. Trade marketing employs strategies such as product assortment optimization and a variety of promotional activities.

Effective trade marketing practices involve understanding buyer behavior and providing an efficient and cost-effective distribution channel. A good trade marketing strategy involves a comprehensive analysis of the target market and an understanding of the wholesale buyer's and retailer's needs. Comprehensive pricing strategy, correct positioning of products, and analysis-supported decisions reduce costs and increase sales.

Creating a comprehensive trade marketing strategy requires careful segmentation. By breaking up the big picture into key elements, such as promotional plans and pricing objectives, trade marketing activities can be thoroughly planned and monitored. It should be noted that trade marketing is not limited to selling directly to retailers—activities can also be aimed at other major influencers such as brokers, wholesalers, distributors, and end consumers.

Aiming promotional activities at each segment of the distribution network requires targeted communication. A good trade marketing plan utilizes marketing tactics such as trade promotions, product launches, sales training, and non-traditional marketing tactics. By understanding the target market and focusing activities on the right locations, trade marketing activities can reap greater rewards.

Finally, it is vital to assess the results of trade marketing activities to make sure they are effective. Analyzing sales and competitive market data at each level of the channel is one of the best ways to keep campaigns on track and adjust strategies when needed.

In summary, trade marketing is a crucial component of any business. It allows manufacturers to build strong relationships with retailers and other partners and ensure that products remain competitive and profitable. Trade marketing is a complex process, involving effective segmentation and analysis of target markets, and an understanding of buyer behavior. By creating comprehensive plans and monitoring results, trade marketing activities can reap greater rewards.

XXIII
Retail Marketing

Retail marketing is a powerful tool for businesses to reach their target customers and increase sales. It involves creating a strategy to promote products and services in a retail setting. This strategy should include a combination of traditional and digital marketing tactics, such as in-store displays, promotional events, and online advertising.

Retail marketing is all about creating an engaging experience for customers. It should be tailored to the target audience and focus on creating a positive customer experience. This can be done through creating an inviting atmosphere, offering discounts and promotions, and providing helpful customer service.

In addition to creating an engaging experience, retail marketing should also focus on building relationships with customers. This can be done through loyalty programs, customer surveys, and personalized emails. By building relationships with customers, businesses can create a sense of loyalty and trust, which can lead to increased sales.

Finally, retail marketing should also focus on creating a memorable brand. This can be done through creating a unique logo, slogan, and other branding elements. By creating a memorable brand, businesses can create a lasting impression on customers and increase brand recognition.

Retail marketing is an essential part of any business's marketing strategy. By creating an engaging experience, building relationships with customers, and creating a memorable brand, businesses can increase sales and reach their target customers. With the right strategy, retail marketing can be a powerful tool for businesses to unlock the secrets of modern marketing.

XXIV
Event Marketing

Event marketing is a powerful tool for businesses to reach their target audience and create a lasting impression. It involves creating an event that is tailored to the needs of the target audience and designed to capture their attention. Event marketing can be used to promote a product, service, or brand, and can be used to create a memorable experience for attendees

Event marketing is a great way to engage with potential customers and build relationships. It can be used to create a buzz around a product or service, and to generate interest in a brand. Events can be used to educate customers about a product or service, and to create a sense of community around a brand. Events can also be used to generate leads and increase sales.

Event marketing can be used to create a unique experience for attendees. Events can be used to create a sense of excitement and anticipation, and to create a memorable experience for attendees. Events can also be used to create a sense of exclusivity and to create a sense of belonging. Events can also be used to create a sense of urgency and to encourage attendees to take action.

Event marketing can be used to create a lasting impression on attendees. Events can be used to create a memorable experience that will stay with attendees long after the event has ended. Events can also be used to create a sense of loyalty and to create a sense of connection with the brand.

Event marketing is an effective way to reach a target audience and create a lasting impression. It involves creating an event that is tailored to the needs of the target audience and designed to capture their attention. Event marketing can be used to promote a product, service, or brand, and can be used to create a memorable experience for attendees. By creating an event that is tailored to the needs of the target audience, businesses can create a lasting impression and build relationships with potential customers.

XXV

Brand Activation and Experiential Marketing

Brand activation and experiential marketing are two of the most powerful tools in a modern marketer's toolbox. Brand activation is the process of creating an emotional connection between a brand and its customers. It involves creating experiences that are memorable and engaging, and that leave a lasting impression on the customer. Experiential marketing, on the other hand, is the practice of creating experiences that are designed to engage customers and create a lasting connection with the brand.

Brand activation and experiential marketing are both essential components of a successful marketing strategy. By creating experiences that are memorable and engaging, brands can create a strong emotional connection with their customers. This connection can lead to increased brand loyalty, higher customer satisfaction, and ultimately, increased sales.

Experiential marketing is also an effective way to reach new customers. By creating experiences that are unique and engaging, brands can attract new customers and create a lasting impression. Experiential marketing can also be used to create a sense of community among customers, which can lead to increased customer loyalty and brand recognition.

Brand activation and experiential marketing are both powerful tools for modern marketers. By creating experiences that are memorable and engaging, brands can create a strong emotional connection with their customers. This connection can lead to increased brand loyalty, higher customer satisfaction, and ultimately, increased sales. Experiential marketing can also be used to reach new customers and create a sense of community among customers. By leveraging the power of brand activation and experiential marketing, modern marketers can unlock the secrets of modern marketing and create a successful marketing strategy.

Other Books Of The Author

1. The Moments When I Met God
2. Kashiyile Theertha Pathangal
3. GURU GYAN VANI
4. Abhiprerak Gita
5. ASSI SE JAIN GHAT TAK
6. Hopelessness of Arjuna
7. The Soul and It's True Nature
8. Sense of Action (Karma)
9. Action through Wisdom
10. Action through Wisdom
11. THEORY AND PRACTICAL OF EVERY ACTION
12. LOGICAL UNDERSTANDING OF THE SUPREME
13. THE IMPERISHABLE SUPREME
14. Yatra Nishadraj se Hanuman Ghat Tak
15. Yatra Karnatak Ghat se Raja Ghat Tak
16. Yatra Pandey Ghat se Prayagraj Ghat Tak
17. Yatra Ranjendra Prasad Ghat se Dattatreya Ghat Tak
18. YaatraSindhiya Ghat se Gwaliar Ghat Tak
19. Yatra Mangala Gauri Ghat se Hanuman Gadhi Ghat Tak
20. Yatra Gaay Ghat Se Nishad Ghat Tak
21. MAA GANGA, GHATEN EVM UTSAV
22. Ganga Arti Dev Deepavali evam Any Utsav
23. Potentials of Digitalized India
24. VEDIC CONSCIOUSNESS
25. A Brief Introduction to Vedic Science
26. Kashi ke Barah Jyotirling
27. IMPACT OF MOTIVATION
28. Let's have a Milky Way Journey
29. Color Therapy in a Nutshell

30. Rigveda in a Nutshell
31. Yajurveda in a Nutshell
32. Samveda in a Nutshell
33. Atharva Veda in a Nutshell
34. Ayushman Bhava - Ayurveda
35. Srimad Bhagavad Gita and Upanishad Connection
36. Srimad Bhagavad Gita - an attempt to summarize each chapter.
37. Facts and Impact of Nakshatra
38. Astro Gems - NAVARATNA
39. Ekadashi - A Concise Overview
40. A Concise View of Hanuman Chalisa
41. Inspirational Gita
42. Nakshatraranyam
43. Summary of 18 Mahapuranas
44. Synopsis of 18 Upa Puranas
45. Rigvediya Upanishads
46. Shukla Yajurvediya Upanishads
47. Krishna Yajurvediya Upanishads
48. Samavediya Upanishads
49. Atharvavediya Upanishads
50. The Seven Great Sages
51. From Rocket Scientist to President Dr. APJ Abdul Kalam
52. The Visionary's Voice - Quotes of Dr. APJ Abdul Kalam
53. The Wisdom of Swami Vivekananda: Insights and Inspiration from a Legendary Spiritual Teacher
54. Ayurvedic Remedies from the Garden
55. Sages and Seers
56. Rising Strong – Motivational Stories of Women
57. Beyond Flames -Mystery stories of Funeral Ghat Manikarnika
58. The Origins of Tulsi: A Look at the Mythological Roots of the Plant"

59. The Holistic Cow: A Look at the Physical, Spiritual, and Cultural Importance of Cows in India
60. Arts of Healing
61. Exploring the Divine
62. Understanding Five Elements
63. The Etymology of Ram
64. Symbols of India
65. Voice of Change (About Speeches of Great Men)
66. She Speaks (About Speeches of Great Women)
67. Patriotism on Celluloid – Brief About Patriotic Films
68. The Music of Motivation: A Brief Guide to Inspirational Film Songs
69. **Unlocking the Secrets of the Dashopanishads**
70. A Cultural Mosaic
71. Ancient Traditions, Modern Minds
72. Ecos of Ancient Wisdom
73. Beneath the Surface
74. From Temples to Ashrams
75. Sages of the Subcontinent
76. The Art of Healling (Ayurveda, Yoga & Naturopathy)
77. Indian Kitchen
78. The Festivals of India
79. The Indian Epics Retold
80. The Power of Mantras
81. The Indian River Ganges
82. The Indian Architecture
83. Rites of Passage
84. The Indian Silk Road
85. The Indian Literature
86. The Indian Villages
87. The Indian Folks & Crafts
88. The Way of Buddha
89. The Ramayan of Tulsidas

90. Astrological Remedies
91. The Secret Power of Motivation
92. Secret of Developing your Inner Strength
93. The Secret Path to Motivation
94. The Art and Secret of Positive Thinking
95. The Secrets of Practicing Ethical Living
96. Indian Art and Painting
97. The Indian Herbalism
98. Bharatanatyam to Kathak
99. Exploring India's Astrological Remedies
100. The Indian Festival of Flowers
101. Indian Handicrafts
102. The Splashes of Joy – India's Colour Festival
103. The Indian Science of Astrology
104. The Indian Mythology
105. Path to Enlightenment
106. The Indian Spirituality for Children
107. Aromas of India
108. The Secrets of Healthy Relationships
109. Ancestral Ties
110. The Indian Street Food
111. Discovering America
112. The Indian Textile
113. Listening to Motivational Speeches
114. Taste of India
115. A Cultural Journey through Indian Nuptials
116. Motivational Quote for Change
117. Secret Strategies for Making Money
118. Secrets to Cultivate a Positive Mindset
119. A Tapestry of Cultures: Exploring India from Kashmir to Kanyakumari
120. Achieving Your Dreams with Resilience: Secret Strategies for Overcoming Obstacles

121. Innovative Startups - 25 Startup Ideas to Spark Your Business Creativity
122. Export Management: Strategies for Global Success
123. Exporting from India - A Step by Step Guide
124. Finance Fundamentals: Mastering Financial Management for Business Success
125. Global Growth Strategies for International Business Development
126. Marketing Mastery: Unlocking the Secrets of Modern Marketing
127. Operations Mastery: Managing the Flow of Value in Business
128. Strategic Business Management: Navigating the Modern Business Landscape
129. Human Resource Management Strategies for Building and Managing a High Performance Team

CONTACT

DR. JAGADEESH PILLAI

MBA & PhD in Vedic Science

Four Times Guinness World Record Holder

Winner of Mahatma Gandhi Vishwa Shanti Puraskar and Global Peace Ambassador

Gemology, Astro & Vastu Consultant - Spiritual Counselor

Consultant for designing World Record Ideas

Efficient Tarot Card Reader

9839093003

myrichindia@gmail.com

drjagadeeshpillai@facebook

drjagadeeshpillai@instagram
jagadeeshpillai@youtube

www. JAGADEESHPILLAI.com

|| LOKAHA SAMASTHAHA SUKHINO BHAVANTU ||

Printed by Libri Plureos GmbH in Hamburg,
Germany